The First Easter

Sally Ann Wright and Angela Jolliffe

Everyone loved Jesus. They came out to cheer when Jesus went with his friends to Jerusalem. They waved palm branches and called out, 'Hooray for Jesus! Jesus is our King!' They made a path for his donkey to walk on.

Everyone loved Jesus because he told people about how much God loved them. He healed people who were ill. He made time for everyone, the grandmas and the little children, people who had no other friends.

One of his friends was called Judas. He knew that Jesus had enemies – people who wanted bad things to happen to him. And Judas was greedy.

'Give me thirty silver coins – and I will take your soldiers to arrest Jesus when it's dark,' said Judas.

Judas went to find Jesus and his other friends with the coins jingling in his pocket.

Jesus and his twelve friends met to eat together in a room in Jerusalem. But Jesus already knew this would be the last meal he would eat with his friends. And he knew what Judas had done.

'One of you has made friends with my enemies,' said Jesus sadly.

No one could believe it. They all agreed with Peter - 'It's not me!' he said.

Jesus broke some bread and shared it with them.

'This is my body,' he said. He drank some wine and shared it. 'This is my blood.'

It was night-time when Jesus took his friends with him into a garden of olive trees to ask God to help him.

While Jesus prayed, Judas came with soldiers through the trees. Jesus let them take him away while all his friends ran and hid.

Peter followed, hiding in the shadows. He waited outside the place where men asked Jesus questions.

'I know you – you're one of his friends,' a girl said.

'No!' said Peter. 'Not me!'
'Yes, you are,' said another.
'No, no! You're wrong!' Peter said, now very afraid.
'You even talk like him,' said another, coming closer.
'No, NO. I am not that man's friend!' said Peter.
Then the rooster crowed. It was morning. What had Peter done?

Pontius Pilate was an important man. He must choose: should Jesus go free? Should he be killed?

He stood in front of a big crowd of people.

'What do you want me to do with Jesus?' Pilate asked them.

'Crucify him!' shouted the people. 'Crucify him!'

The people who had paid Judas had also paid people in the crowd. Pilate gave Jesus to his soldiers.

They teased Jesus cruelly. They put a crown of sharp thorns on his head.

'Long live the King!' they laughed.

Then Jesus' enemies put him to death on a cross. The soldiers laughed and played games with dice.

Two thieves were crucified with him. Jesus asked God to forgive them and everyone in the whole world for all the bad and unkind things that anyone had ever done.

Jesus' mother, Mary, was there. She felt very, very sad.

'My friend John will look after you,' said Jesus quietly.

Then there was a rumbling earthquake. The sun went in and the sky turned dark, even though it was the middle of the day.

Then Jesus died. It was the saddest day there had ever been.

Later that day, a rich man called Joseph, who had been a friend of Jesus, carried Jesus' body to his own quiet and beautiful garden.

Joseph had spoken bravely to Pilate himself.

'Yes, now he is dead, you may take Jesus away to bury him,' said Pilate to Joseph.

Another friend of Jesus, Nicodemus, helped Joseph. The two friends gently laid Jesus in a cool, dark, rocky cave and pushed a very big and heavy stone across the doorway. Nobody could possibly get in or out now.

Jesus' mother, Mary, and some other friends came to the quiet garden too.

They were very, very sad, because they knew they would never see Jesus again.

Then ... very early on Sunday morning, Mary Magdalene and her friends went to the garden, to the place where Jesus was buried.

But the cave was empty – the big and heavy stone had been rolled away! What could have happened?

Two angels shone beside the cave.

'Jesus is alive again!' said the angels.

Then, while Mary was trying to understand what they could mean, she saw someone in the garden through her tears, someone who spoke her name ... Someone who was Jesus - and he really was alive!

Jesus went to see his friends that same day but Thomas was not there with them. So when they told him that Jesus was alive, Thomas could not believe them.

'I need to see his hands and feet,' said Thomas.

'But Jesus is alive!' said his friends. 'Really, truly alive! Mary has seen him. We have seen him!'

'But I need to see him too. I need to touch the places where the soldiers hurt him,' said Thomas.

A few days later Jesus suddenly appeared in a room where all his friends were together. This time, Thomas was there too.

'Peace be with you,' smiled Jesus.

Then he said to Thomas:

'Look at me, Thomas. Touch my wounds for yourself.'

'It really IS you!' said Thomas in wonder. 'You are my Lord and my God!'

Peter and his friends went fishing one night, out on Lake Galilee - but they couldn't catch any fish at all. They felt tired and disappointed and grumpy.

'Try again!' called a voice from the water's edge.

This time they caught a huge number of wriggling fish. They could hardly pull in the net!

'It's Jesus!' said the friends.

'Come and eat,' said Jesus as they dragged in the fish.

Jesus had made a little fire and they all had breakfast of fish and bread. It tasted good!

Then Jesus said to Peter: 'I want you to do something special for me, Peter. Love me and follow me, and take care of all my friends.'

Then Peter knew that Jesus had forgiven him for saying he didn't know him at all.

Before Jesus went back to be with God in Heaven, he told his friends he would always be with them.

'Go to Jerusalem and wait till the Holy Spirit comes,' he told them.

It was the feast of Pentecost. Suddenly there was a rushing wind blowing through the whole room. There were bright little flames everywhere that touched everyone.

Then Jesus' friends began to speak in other languages. Now they could tell everyone about what Jesus had done for them!

'Jesus is God's Son,' said Peter. 'He came to earth to die for us. He's alive again, and he will forgive everything anyone has done wrong. And his Spirit will help us to love other people and to live the way he wants us to.'

First edition 2021

Published by Authentic Media Ltd
PO Box 6326, Bletchley,
Milton Keynes, MK1 9GG
www.authenticmedia.co.uk

Copyright © 2021 Anno Domini Publishing
www.ad-publishing.com

Text copyright © 2021 Sally Ann Wright
Illustrations copyright © 2013 Angela Jolliffe

Publishing Director: Annette Reynolds
Art Director: Gerald Rogers
Pre-production Manager: Kev Holt

All rights reserved

Printed in China